Marilyn

BY CINDY DE LA HOZ

RUNNING PRESS
PHILADELPHIA • LONDON

Library of Congress Control Number: 2008922495

ISBN 978-0-7624-3149-6

Running Press Book Publishers
2300 Chestnut Street
Philadelphia, PA 19103-4371

Visit us on the web!
www.runningpress.com

Contents

With a single photograph or a momentary flash of Marilyn's image on the screen, the movies' platinum legend still captivates audiences half a century after her death. Magnetism; a rare combination of sexiness and vulnerability; and her specialized manner of speaking and carrying herself came together in the creation of a wholly unique personality.

4-1838

While she may have taken inspiration from earlier platinum-locked stars like Jean Harlow, Betty Grable, and Lana Turner, no one had seen anyone like Marilyn when she rose to fame in the early 1950s. Since then, a myriad of imitators have surfaced, but none can capture her spirit.

Marilyn's story is nothing short of fascinating. Norma Jeane Mortensen was fatherless and her mother suffered from mental illness. She found escape at the movies, where the star struck child spent hours watching her screen idols. While working for an aircraft factory during World War II, the beautiful teenager was discovered by a photographer and she became a model. Getting into films was a natural next step.

Contracts with Twentieth Century-Fox, Columbia Pictures, and then back to Fox, led to "Marilyn Monroe" becoming one of Hollywood's greatest stars. Through her own willpower, Marilyn transcended her sexy persona to become an actress of enormous talent, while

her luminous, indefinable quality that separates the actors from the stars defied viewers to look at anyone but her when she was on the screen.

Through images from her films and rare backstage photographs, intriguing morsels of her greatness are served up in this mini celebration. With a camera subject as enthralling as Marilyn, it's not size that matters.

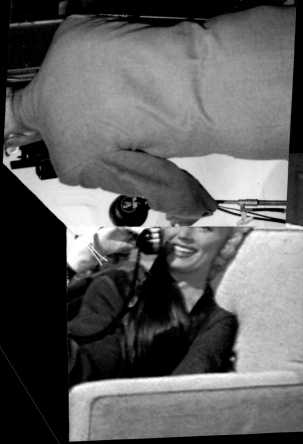

NAME:

Norma Jeane Mortensen,
legally changed to Marilyn
Monroe in 1956

BIRTH DATE:
June 1, 1926, at 9:30 a.m.

BIRTHPLACE:
Los Angeles General Hospital

MOTHER:
Gladys Baker

FATHER:

Gladys had been married to Martin Edward Mortensen, hence the last name on Norma Jeane's birth certificate. Marilyn believed her father to be Charles Stanley Gifford, a co-worker of Gladys's at Consolidated Film Industries, where Gladys worked as a film cutter. Most biographies concur with this.

SIBLINGS:

Half-sister, Berniece Miracle, and half-brother, Hermitt Jack Baker, Gladys's children with first husband Jack Baker

EYES:

Blue

HAIR:

Her natural color was reddish brown, but it was lightened to every shade from warm honey to white blonde—and she always parted her hair on the right side.

31

HEIGHT:
5 feet, 5 inches

SHOE SIZE:
7AA

DRESS SIZE:
12, on average. Accounting for changes in calculations, that's about a size 4, perhaps 6, today.

WEIGHT:
Generally maintained between 115 and 120 pounds. She weighed in at 140 at her heaviest, in 1960.

MARRIAGES
James Dougherty (1942 to 1946)
Joe DiMaggio (1954)
Arthur Miller (1956 to 1961)

DEATH:

August 4, 1962, at 12305 Fifth
Helene Drive, her home in
Brentwood, California. She was
thirty-six.

. . . .

FINAL RESTING PLACE:

Westwood Village Memorial
Park Cemetery

favorites

ACTORS

Clark Gable
Marlon Brando
Montgomery Clift
Cary Grant
Charlie Chaplin

44

ACTRESSES

Jean Harlow

Joan Crawford

Marie Dressler

Greta Garbo

Betty Grable

Ginger Rogers

Norma Shearer

FOODS:
Caviar, steak, hotdogs

DRINK:
Dom Pérignon 1953

SOFT DRINK:
Ginger Ale

47

SHOE DESIGNER:
Salvatore Ferragamo

MALE SINGER:
Frank Sinatra

FEMALE SINGER:
Ella Fitzgerald

COLORS:

Black, white, red, beige

BOOKS:

The Little Prince
  by Antoine de Saint Exupéry

How Stanislavsky Directs
  by Michael Gorchakov

The Rights of Man
  by Thomas Paine

Abraham Lincoln
  by Carl Sandburg

RESTAURANTS:

Romanoff's, La Scala

ARTISTS:

Michelangelo, Boticelli,
El Greco, Goya, Picasso,
Leonardo da Vinci,
Fra Angelico, Rodin

PERFUME:

Chanel No. 5

Dostoevsky,
George Bernard Shaw, J. D.
Salinger, Tennessee Williams,
Colette, William Shakespeare,
Thomas Wolfe, Marcel Proust,
Walt Whitman, John Keats,
Gerard Manley Hopkins

ROLE:
Grushenka in Dostoevsky's
The Brothers Karamazov

by Tennessee Wil

ACTING COACHES:
Michael Chekhov
Natasha Lytess
Lee Strasberg
Paula Strasberg

BEST FRIEND:
The telephone

PET:

Maf Honey, a poodle said to be a gift from Frank Sinatra

DISGUISE:

Dark sunglasses, a scarf tied around her chin, and sometimes a dark wig

DRESS:

A low-cut gold lamé gown by William Travilla (pictured)

The Movies

Scudda Hoo! Scudda Hay! (1948)

Dangerous Years (1947)

Ladies of the Chorus (1948)

Love Happy (1950)

A Ticket to Tomahawk (1950)

The Asphalt Jungle (1950)

The Fireball (1950)

Right Cross (1950)

All About Eve (1950)

Hometown Story (1951)

As Young as You Feel (1951)

Love Nest (1951)

Let's Make It Legal (1951)

Clash by Night (1952)

We're Not Married (1952)

Don't Bother to Knock (1952)

Monkey Business (1952)

O. Henry's Full House (1952)

Niagara (*1*953)

Gentlemen Prefer Blondes (1953)

How to Marry a Millionaire (*1*953)

River of No Return (1954)

There's No Business Like Show Business (1954)

The Seven Year Itch (1955)

The Stats

Name:
Norma Jeane Mortensen,
legally changed to Marilyn
Monroe in 1956

Birth date:
June 1, 1926, at 9:30 a.m.

Birthplace:
Los Angeles General Hospital

Mother:
Gladys Baker

Arthur Miller, Fyodor
Dostoevsky, Michael Gorchakov,
George Bernard Shaw, J. D.
Salinger, Tennessee Williams,
Colette, William Shakespeare,
Thomas Wolfe, Marcel Proust,
Walt Whitman, John Keats,
Gerard Manley Hopkins

ROLE:

Grushenka in Dostoevsky's
The Brothers Karamazov

PLAY:

A Streetcar Named Desire
by Tennessee Williams

ACTING COACHES:

Michael Chekhov
Natasha Lytess
Lee Strasberg
Paula Strasberg

BEST FRIEND:

The telephone

- **PET:**

    Maf Honey, a poodle said to be a gift from Frank Sinatra

- **DISGUISE:**

    Dark sunglasses, a scarf tied around her chin, and sometimes a dark wig

- **DRESS:**

    A low-cut gold lamé gown by William Travilla (pictured)

Bus Stop (1956)

The Prince and the Showgirl (1957)

Some Like It Hot (1959)

Let's Make Love (1960)

The Misfits (1961)

Something's Got to Give
(unfinished, 1962)

It took six years after her screen debut to establish that Marilyn was a natural for musicals, but *Gentlemen Prefer Blondes* was worth the wait. Through training with voice coaches including Fred Karger (in early years) and Hal Schaefer (for Fox musicals), she developed a beautiful singing voice with a style as distinctive as everything else about the Marilyn Monroe persona.

Though not a trained dancer, she also had the rhythm necessary for her production numbers. Applying her signature sexiness to the choreography of dance directors like Jack Cole, she created some of the most memorable musical moments captured on film.

In her first musical at Fox, *A Ticket to Tomahawk*, Marilyn danced to "Oh, What a Forward Young Man You Are" with Dan Dailey and chorus girls Barbara Smith, Joyce MacKenzie, and Marion Marshall.

84

Serving as a tribute to Irving Berlin, *There's No Business Like Show Business* showcased a slew of the songwriter's hit tunes, three of which were performed by Marilyn in her inimitable style: "After You Get What You Want You Don't Want It," "Lazy," and "Heat Wave."

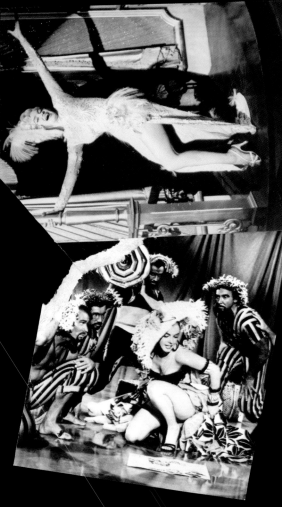

Singing songs by Cole Porter and Jimmy Van Heusen and Sammy Cahn, Marilyn played the star of an off-Broadway show in *Let's Make Love*. Co-starring French entertainer Yves Montand, the movie turned out to be her last musical.

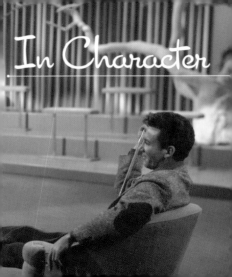

In Character

Scudda Hoo! Scudda Hay! was the first movie that Marilyn worked on (her second to be released to theaters). Her first words in a movie are, "Hi, Rad!" It was a greeting directed at leading lady June Haver.

98

Marilyn frequently played secretaries, pin-ups, dumb blondes, and gold diggers early on, sometimes all at once. While she could be better, and more endearing, in these kinds of parts than anyone else, they only scratched the surface of her talent, as proven by her later films. In movies like *Bus Stop*, *Some*

Like it Hot, and *The Misfits*, she revealed previously unsuspected dimensions of herself and broke our hearts. On the following pages, Marilyn is shown in a few of her well-known character portrayals.

"Miss Caswell is an actress, a graduate of the Copacabana School of Dramatic Art."

"...ney, your father's been so divine with me that sometimes even I feel like calling him 'Daddy.'"

"Oh yes, Mr. Oxly's been complaining about my punctuation, so I'm careful to get here before nine."

"Sure I'm meeting somebody. Just anybody handy—as long as he's a man. How about the ticket seller himself? I could grab him on my way out. Or one of the kids with the phonograph. Anybody suits me— take your pick."

"You know what they say about girls who wear glasses."

"Oh, do you feel the breeze from the subway? Isn't it delicious?"

"I'd like for you
to kiss me, Beau."

115

*Behind
the
Scenes*

It is well known that Marilyn became increasingly difficult to work with. In all fairness, late arrivals to the set and requiring numerous retakes was less a case of a star's unprofessional behavior than an artist's crippling insecurities. But once she overcame her fears and had a camera pointed at her, there was no one

like Marilyn. The images on the following pages show the actress at work behind the scenes at the studio and on location in Canada for *River of No Return*.